To my wife Barbara—the typist, the critic, and the staunch supporter of the learner.

MANAGING WITH PEOPLE

RAYMOND J. BURBY

McDonnell Douglas Corporation
Long Beach, California

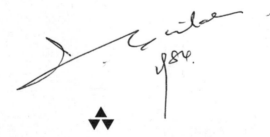

ADDISON-WESLEY PUBLISHING COMPANY, INC.
Reading, Massachusetts · Menlo Park, California
London · Amsterdam · Don Mills, Ontario · Sydney

THIS BOOK IS IN THE ADDISON-WESLEY SERIES
IN SUPERVISORY TRAINING

Second printing, March 1975

ISBN 0-201-00723-1
ABCDEFGHIJ-AL-798765

PREFACE

On the job, as well as anywhere else, every person has reasons for what he does. A man may not know the reasons he has for a particular behavior (they may be subconscious), but they usually have some effect on the way he does his job—and that is the reason for this book. In this book we try to help you understand why people behave as they do on the job and suggest ways of handling on-the-job people problems.

The search for solutions to problems related to human behavior will probably continue as long as man exists, for the combinations of people and conditions affecting human behavior appear endless. However, that should not prevent us from trying to find satisfactory solutions to problems arising from behavior on the job. A good supervisor will find that his skill at handling people problems will grow as each new insight illuminates the next problem, long after the contents of this book have been mastered.

Regarding those contents: they have been reviewed by several people, and the resulting suggestions have made the material more meaningful. For such assistance I am truly grateful.

At the back of this book, on perforated pages, are a Pre-Test and a Post-Test. I would suggest that you tear out the Pre-Test and complete it before you start the course. Don't check the answers, but set the test aside until you have completed the course. After the course has been completed, take the Post-Test. Then score both tests by checking your answers against those provided on the answer sheet, which is also at the back of the book. By comparing the answers to the two tests, you can get an indication of how much you have learned from the course.

I hope that you will learn quite a bit from this book, and I expect that much of what you learn will raise new questions. Concerning the question of why people do as they do on the job, it can truly be said that all knowledge is impossible—but some knowledge is better than none.

Long Beach, California   R.J.B.
March 1968

CONTENTS

NOTE

This is a programed text. When you have selected an answer to a question, turn to the page indicated after the answer you have selected.

If you have selected the right answer, you will be given new material to learn. If you have selected the wrong answer, you will find out why the answer is wrong, and you will be asked to return to the original page to choose a better answer.

At the top of each answer page you will find, in parentheses, the number of the page on which the question appeared. This will help you find you way back and forth in the book.

CHAPTER 1

HUMAN NEEDS

The world about us seems bountiful, but it is actually a world of scarcity; too often there seems not to be enough of everything to meet the needs of mankind. Man reacts to what is around him, and so he tries to reshape the world to satisfy *his needs* or what he believes to be *the needs of others*.

This is a physical world, and certain of man's physical needs must be satisfied if he is to exist. This is just as true today as it was thousands of years ago, when early man lived in caves.

But man is a creature of mind, also, and so he has mental needs as well as physical needs. Once man has the things that keep him warm and free from hunger, he finds other needs, both physical and mental, that have to be satisfied. And though they may not be basic, these needs can be very compelling.

The needs listed below are ranked in order of (1) most important, (2) next most important, and so on. Which of the rankings, A, B, or C, most accurately lists man's physical needs in order of importance?

A. (1) Food, (2) car, (3) house, (4) radio, (5) water. . . Page 4

B. (1) House, (2) water, (3) food, (4) radio, (5) car. . . Page 5

C. (1) Water, (2) food, (3) house, (4) car, (5) radio. . . Page 6

Did you read the note before Chapter 1? You are probably so used to turning to the next page while reading a book that you quite naturally did it this time.

This book doesn't work that way. Instead, each time you answer a question, you should proceed directly to the page that is indicated beside your answer.

Your answer: A. Food, car, house, radio, water.

We do not think this is the best listing of the priority of man's needs. Perhaps you are hungry at this moment, so food is topmost on your list of needs. But suppose the radio just brought you the announcement that due to circumstances beyond anyone's control the water supply for a hundred miles around had been destroyed?

In most instances you can do without almost anything but water, then food, then warmth.

Please return and select a better answer.

Your answer: B. House, water, food, radio, car.

We think there is a better priority list than the one you chose. It is possible that the biggest slice of your earnings at present is going to mortgage payments or rent. But does this mean that men must have housing before they respond to any other need?

Let us suppose the radio just brought you the announcement that water would no longer be available within a hundred miles of your house. In most circumstances man's first need is water, then food, then warmth, etc.

Please return; there is a better answer.

Your answer: C. Water, food, house, car, radio.

Correct. Surely this is the best listing of man's physical needs in order of priority. Because of his physical nature, man must have water before anything else, then food, then shelter. After these he needs transportation and communication. As you can see, man reacts to the world around him in relation to his needs. First things first.

Today there are many physical needs which man must satisfy before he can do good work. Once the basic needs mentioned above are taken care of, others arise. Some of them, such as good lighting, clean work areas, desks, and machines are usually provided by the employer.

Very often we don't realize that a need exists until the thing that fills that need fails to work or is lost. Let's say, for example, that you work at a desk that is provided with a lamp. One day the bulb burns out. You immediately realize that you need more light, and it is up to you to take some action that will fulfill that need. Therefore you will most likely:

1. Go to the water cooler for a drink . . . . Page 7

2. Phone plant maintenance . . . . Page 8

3. Call in a secretary and dictate a memo to your boss, telling him that you need a light . . . . Page 11

Your answer: 1. Go to the water cooler for a drink.

This is not the correct answer. Maybe you are bored with what you are doing and would be glad to have the light go out. But going to the water cooler would not be responding to your need for light. Later on in this book we will talk about other factors that affect behavior or actions, but right now we are asking what you would be most likely to do if you felt you needed better lighting.

Please return and select another answer.

Your answer: 2. Phone plant maintenance.

Of course this is the best answer; it is the most direct action of the three choices given. You can be reasonably sure that most people, most of the time, will do what will most quickly, easily, and completely satisfy their needs.

An individual's needs, however, are not all physical; they are also mental. Mental needs are not as easily seen as physical needs, but they can create very powerful demands for satisfaction. When your light went out you could easily see the problem and solve it, but unless you know something about mental needs and how they affect people you may be working in the dark more than you know.

Because of the importance of mental needs and the pressures they create within people, we will spend considerable time examining those mental needs that are most likely to affect a job situation. It will not be a particularly easy task, but it can be very rewarding to you in your own job situation. *Some* of the important mental needs are shown on the next page.

Once man has taken care of his basic physical requirements he may respond to other needs. One important need is for security—that is, protection for water and food supplies, shelter, and the other things man values. And because security can't be felt or seen, we call it a mental need.

Affection is another mental need. It has no physical dimensions, but we know, for instance, that although a newborn child may be well fed, it may sicken and die if it is not handled, petted, spoken to, and loved.

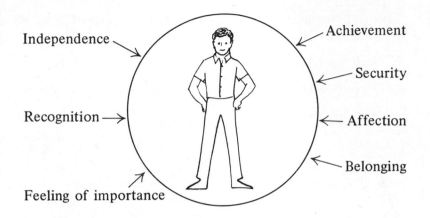

We also need to be accepted by others. That's one reason why people join clubs, or work better when they feel that they belong with a group. Of course, this and the other mental needs mentioned above are just a few of the many that exist.

We have already noted the action taken in response to a physical need for light. Now let us examine a response to a mental need.

Bill and John were considered for promotion to the one foreman's job that was open. Both wanted it for several reasons, one of which was that they felt it showed that the company recognized a man's abilities.

Bill got the promotion.

John's reaction was to resent Bill and do everything he could to interfere with Bill's work objectives. John could have reacted differently; why did he act that way?

Which of the needs listed below do you feel caused John to behave as he did?

1. Need for a better job . . . . Page 12

2. Need for recognition . . . . Page 13

3. Need for security . . . . Page 14

Your answer: 3. Call in a secretary and dictate a memo to your boss telling him that you need a light.

No. This is not the best answer. It could be that in your job situation this is the only way you can get a light, but we hope not!

We gave you three choices and said you were going to behave in a way that would satisfy your need for better lighting. Didn't we offer a better choice than the one you picked?

Please return and select a better answer.

Your answer: 1. Need for a better job.

Nothing in our example indicated that John needed a better job. In all the case histories you study in this book, please consider only the facts given.

Why did John behave as he did when Bill got the promotion? We listed just a few of the many mental needs that exist; they were:

Security   Recognition
Affection   Independence
Achievement   Feeling of importance
Belonging

Ask yourself which of these needs did John feel would have been satisfied if he had gotten the job.

Please return and try again.

Your answer: 2. Need for recognition.

That is correct. You considered the facts given in this case history and drew the best conclusion. It is likely that John's *goal* was a foreman's job because getting the promotion would satisfy his need for recognition. There was nothing in the case history to indicate the John felt any insecurity, probably so John behaved as he did because his need for recognition was being denied.

We can draw a simple illustration of John's behavior and from it we can see that John wanted to satisfy his need for recognition. Not getting recognition, John reacted by behaving in a manner unfriendly to Bill.

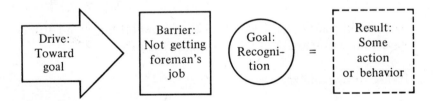

This illustration also brings up another point: that the pressure to satisfy needs can be called a drive. As a matter of fact, pressures to satisfy needs are usually called drives, so that's the word we'll use from here on.

Suppose that we know that a person's need for recognition is very strong. We can safely assume he has a drive to satisfy this need. Being aware of this we can:

1. Better understand his behavior . . . . Page 15

2. Better understand his needs . . . . Page 18

Your answer: 3. Need for security.

No. In our example we did not indicate that either John or Bill was feeling a need for more security.

In all the case histories you study in this book, try to consider only the facts given. While it is good you recognized security as a mental need, it was not the factor in this case study. Here are some of the mental needs we pointed out to you earlier (just a few of all that exist).

Security	Recognition
Affection	Independence
Achievement	Feeling of importance
Belonging	

You might ask yourself which of these mental needs did John have that was frustrated when Bill got the job.

Please return and try again.

Your answer: 1. We can better understand his behavior.

Certainly this is the better answer. A person seeking to satisfy a certain need, say for recognition, will behave in a certain way. Keeping this fact in mind, we carefully observe another person's behavior and find that we can easily understand certain things he does—things that we couldn't understand if we didn't realize that he was trying to satisfy some need.

Take John, for example. Failing to satisfy his need for recognition, he sulked; he couldn't make himself do as well as he should. If we knew he needed recognition and had failed to get it, we would understand why he was sulking and look for some other way to satisfy his need. The result would be much better work from John.

A theory of human needs has been developed by A. H. Maslow,* who suggested that man satisfies his needs in order, from the lowest (survival) to the highest level (creativity).

				Creativity
			Self-esteem	Achievement, realization of full potential
		Environment	Skills, ability, knowledge, productivity, importance.	
	Security	(social)		
Survival	Insurance, social security, law and order	Home, church clubs, friends, marriage		
Bodily needs				
←———— Insecurity ————→		←———— Feeling of well-being ————→		

*Maslow, A.H., *Motivation and Personality,* Harper and Brothers, New York (1954).

Notice that until man has satisfied his needs for survival and safety he is insecure. It is only after those needs have been taken care of that man has a feeling of well-being and can go on to satisfy his higher-level needs. Keep in mind, also, that the drive to satisfy a need usually lasts just as long as the need exists.

Drives tend to move people to do certain things. You may not like some of these things, but it might be well to find out the reason behind them (if possible) before stopping them. Suppose you tell someone, "Don't shout at the men. They shouldn't be bullied." The man you're speaking to may stop shouting—and find some quieter way to bully the men. You see, unless you can find out *why* he bullies others—and do something about it—the problem will still be with you.

Removing the opportunity to satisfy a need does *not* remove the need itself, you know. Suppose a company has allowed its employees a 10-minute coffee break in the afternoon, then cancels that coffee break. If the employees feel they need that break, taking it away from them will not cancel the need. It's a safe bet that they will find a way to get around the change in policy.

Let's examine a few case histories that show some of the ways people behave to satisfy their needs.

Al, a lathe operator, figured out a new way to turn out a part that he thought would save the company time and money. When he felt the time was right, he told his foreman about it. The foreman got very angry at Al and said "Don't spend your time getting bright ideas around here. I'll do the thinking; you just run your damned lathe like everybody else!

The foreman probably behaved this way because:

1. He felt that Al should have put the idea in the suggestion box, so that it would have been evaluated independently of his opinion. . . . . Page 19

2. He had a strong need for the feeling of achievement, so he believed that he could satisfy *all* the shop's requirements.

   . . . . Page 20

3. He wanted Al to think only of the production schedule, upon which the foreman's job security depended. Page 21

Your answer: 2. Better understand his needs.

This is only half an answer.

If you realize that people have more than one mental need, that's good. We know people have various needs, but knowing of a person's need for recognition does not tell us much about his other needs.

On the other hand, knowing about a person's need for recognition might help us understand his behavior. John sulks when he misses a promotion. This isn't like John, normally, so his behavior tends to tell us that he wants the company to recognize his abilities. Recognition is a very important factor to John.

Please return to page 13.

Your answer: 1. He felt that Al should have put the idea in the suggestion box, so that it would have been evaluated independently of his opinion.

No. If this were the case we suspect the foreman would have said so instead of behaving in such an angry fashion.

Please return and try again.

Your answer: 2. He had a strong need for the feeling of achievement.

Right. The foreman needed to feel that he was the one who achieved things in that department. Al's idea conflicted with this need and made the foreman feel less than completely competent. The foreman did not behave in the best way, of course, and this sort of treatment is bound to create a "who cares" attitude in any shop.

Now let's review that case history and take a look at Al's behavior. Al is a lathe operator. He figured out a new way to turn out a part that he thought would save the company time and money. When he thought the time was right, he went to the foreman and told him what he had done.

We already know what the foreman's behavior was. But why did Al, on his very own, figure out a new way to produce a part?

1. His regular job did not provide for independent action
    . . . . Page 22

2. He had a desire for affection . . . . Page 23

3. Figuring out a new way to make a part satisfied Al's
    need for a feeling of achievement . . . . Page 24

Your answer: 3. He wanted Al to think only of the production schedule, upon which the foreman's job security depended.

No, this isn't right. The foreman gave no indication that Al was not meeting a production mark. Even if this were true, Al, in presenting a new idea that could speed production, would enhance the foreman's job security, not threaten it. It would scarcely bring about such an angry reaction.

Please return and try again.

Your answer: 1. Al's regular job did not provide for independent action.

That's not correct. Al figured out how to produce a part which might save production time. Surely that was independent action. And if he felt a need for independence, would he go to his boss with his idea? Ask yourself just what drove Al to do what he did. What need was he satisfying by seeking better methods?

Please return and find a better answer.

Your answer: 2. Al had a desire for affection.

This is not the best answer. If affection was Al's need, he could have satisfied it better with other activity—for example, by lending a hand to other lathe operators in his group. At the very least he would probably talk over his idea with the other fellows in the shop and it would have been common knowledge that Al was working on an idea. Ask yourself just what drove Al to do what he did.

Please return and find a better answer.

Your answer: 3. Figuring out a new way to make a part satisfied Al's need for a feeling of achievement.

Of course! Al's job was challenging enough to cause him to try to help production. He was reacting to a need to achieve this goal. If the foreman had told Al he'd check into his idea, Al would have been rewarded and his need to achieve would have been satisfied.

The interesting point in the interplay between these two individuals is that both had a primary need to achieve. We had an opportunity here to stand outside the action, as it were, and see how the needs of individuals can conflict and affect results in a negative way.

Here is another case.

Mary was hired for her skill in using her hands. After the first few days of training she was able to put together complicated subassemblies at about twice the rate of normal shop

production. However, when she was moved into the production line, which consisted of about 50 women assemblers, she was ridiculed by those around her for high turnout. Her rate dropped rapidly, and she then continued to produce at about the shop average.

Mary had the ability to produce at a much higher rate than the group average. Which reason is most likely to have caused her to cut her production?

1. She wanted to be liked . . . . Page 26

2. She saw that everyone was getting paid the same rate regardless of achievement . . . . Page 28

3. She only turned out a lot of work in the beginning to be sure of getting the job . . . . Page 29

Your answer: 1. Mary wanted to be liked.

That's correct; Mary needed affection. The evidence shows that Mary could do much better work and had more than enough skill to satisfy any needs she might have for recognition, security, or achievement. But her need for affection was strongest, and she changed her behavior when her skill failed to win her affection from her fellow workers.

You've done well to come this far, nearly to the end of our chapter on Human Needs. Before we close the chapter, though, we'd like to examine one more very interesting fact about the subject: Human needs are endless, because *when one need is satisfied, another need arises.*

This means that when you recognize someone's need and take steps to satisfy it, you shouldn't expect the satisfaction to last forever. Soon a new need will require satisfaction, or perhaps the old one will have to be reinforced. If a man is working very hard for recognition, you might satisfy his need by giving him a raise. Then he will be happy. But for how long? Once he has achieved recognition he may then develop a need for affection—to be popular among the men he works with. Or eventually the need for recognition may crop up again, requiring the reinforcement of another raise. You can depend on it, then; when one need is satisfied, another need arises (or the same one eventually comes up again).

It's time now for a brief review of our study of human needs. There are two types of human needs, the most basic of which is the physical type. A human being *must* have water, he *must* have food, and even in the mildest climates he *must* have some sort of shelter. Man's body has to be nourished and protected.

Now, what is the other type of needs man has?

1. Bodily needs . . . . Page 30

2. Mental needs . . . . Page 31

3. I don't remember . . . . Page 32

Your answer: 2. Mary saw that everyone was getting paid the same rate regardless of achievement.

Not very likely. This might have been the attitude among some of the women assemblers; why work hard for the same pay? But Mary liked her work and was skilled at it. She didn't have to work harder than the others to produce more.

If Mary continued to produce more than the others in the group, what might be their reaction toward her?

Please return and select a better answer.

Your answer: 3. Mary only turned out a lot of work in the beginning to be sure of getting the job.

This is not very likely. Mary was chosen for her ability to do the type of work required. She was highly skilled at this type of work and there is no indication that she had to try very hard to master the job. And if security was such an important need to Mary, wouldn't she produce more to keep the job, instead of lowering her output?

Please return and select a better answer.

Your answer: 1. Bodily needs.

Not correct. Did you misread the question? We wanted to know what type of needs people have *besides* bodily needs. The answer, of course, is mental needs.

Please continue on page 31.

Your answer: 2 Mental needs.

Right. Can you recall our illustration of Maslow's theory of human needs? It suggests that from the lowest level to the highest, human needs may be arranged in the following order: survival, security, social, self-esteem and creativity.

At which levels on this ascending scale of needs did Maslow indicate that people were insecure?

1. Survival and social . . . . .Page 33

2. Survival and security . . . . .Page 34

3. Survival and self-esteem .Page 36

Your answer: 3. I don't remember.

O.K., glad to see you are honest. The needs people have besides bodily or physical needs are called mental needs. An easy way to remember mental needs is by recalling the picture you saw awhile ago.

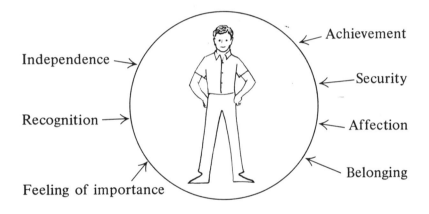

All the above, security, achievement, recognition, etc., are considered mental needs.

Please continue on page 31.

Your answer: 1. Survival and social.

No. This is an easy mistake to make. Of course, people do band together as a social unit and so you came quite naturally to the answer you chose. However, closer examination shows that this banding together is a response to the need for survival and security.

It is safe to assume that no one can feel secure while trying to survive and that no one can satisfy social needs until they are secure. Survival has to be assured, then security. That is why Maslow feels that until the needs of these two levels are satisfied, man is insecure.

Please proceed to page 34.

Your answer: 2. Survival and security.

You are correct. As long as we have to struggle to survive or to obtain law and order, we are insecure. When our security is no longer threatened, we can turn our attention to higher-level needs.

This is not to say that higher-level needs are completely absent or unfelt before survival and security are assured. We know that the cave man decorated his dwelling while his survival was still a pretty nip-and-tuck affair. We also know that his drawings were quite crude, while his arrowheads were rather skillfully finished. Even though his creative needs were being fulfilled, primitive man still gave most of his attention to the problem of survival. First things first.

By now we know that every individual has needs, and that at any given moment, one or more of these needs are pressing him for satisfaction. But just what other knowledge does this give us?

Your answer: 3. Survival and self-esteem.

Sorry, no. Self-esteem is a luxury one cannot afford when faced with the need to survive. To put it bluntly, if the alternative were certain death, no one would hesitate to escape from a burning house in their underwear, no matter how strongly they might object to being seen in public that way under normal conditions.

The levels of insecurity are the need for survival and the need for security. Until these needs are satisfied, higher needs, such as the need for self-esteem, cannot be fulfilled.

Please continue on page 34.

Your answer: 1. It shows that every individual has a physical need or a mental need, or perhaps both.

No. We already know that all people have needs which must be satisfied. The question was, what might it mean to us to know this?

Sometimes one need cries out for satisfaction more insistently than the others. This presses the individual to some action or behavior that will satisfy that need. Simply knowing this fact can tell us something about a person's behavior, and understanding the behavior helps us to understand the person.

Please continue to page 39.

Your answer: 2. It shows that an individual has more than one need to be satisfied.

No. The question was, what might it mean to us to know about these needs? We should already know that people have more than one need to be satisfied. When one need is stronger than the others, a person will be pressed into some action or behavior to satisfy it. Knowing this can tell us something about a person's behavior, and a person's behavior can tell us something about the person.

Please continue to page 39.

Your answer: 3. It shows that knowing a person's needs might explain something about his behavior.

Yes, that's correct. Let's illustrate that point with this example. Tom needs transportation, and so he is going to buy a car. Dick tells him that he should buy an inexpensive model, because that will do the job well enough. Harry says nothing, because he knows something about Tom that Dick doesn't know; he knows that Tom needs recognition as well as transportation, so he has an idea what to expect.

When Tom shows up in a brand new Supersonic 8, with gold-plated muffler and power-assisted horn button, Dick is surprised and a little irritated that his friend didn't take his advice. Not Harry, though. He knows that even though Tom will have to make extra sacrifices to pay for the car, it is worthwhile to Tom to be able to satisfy his need for transportation and his need for recognition at the same time.

One final question. What happens when a need is satisfied?

1. The drive for that need is reduced . . . . .Page 40

2. Another need becomes important . . . . .Page 41

3. Both the above occur . . . . .Page 42

Your answer: 2. The drive for that need is reduced.

That is true, but the better answer is 3, both occur.

When the drive toward satisfaction of one need is reduced, the drive toward another need has room to develop. Thus a new need takes highest priority. It is for this reason that people seem never to be completely satisfied.

Please continue now to page 43.

Your answer: 1. Another need becomes important.

That is true, but the better answer is 3, both occur.

When one need is satisfied its importance is indeed reduced. However, another need becomes important. It is for this reason that people seem never to be completely satisfied.

Please continue now to page 43.

Your answer: 3. Both occur.

Very good. Each of the first two statements answers the question in part; together they form the complete answer.

You understand that when something has satisfied a need, the drive for that need is reduced. When one need is satisfied, another need takes priority, and the drive for its fulfillment begins to have a noticeable affect on the person whose need it is.

In the next chapter we will discuss motivation.

Please proceed to page 43.

Complete this brief test and then turn to the next page to
check your answers. If you miss any of these questions, you
can review the subject by going back to the pages indicated
after the answers.

1. Man has two kinds of needs. These are called
   _____ needs and _____ needs.

2. Man's efforts to satisfy his needs result in some sort of
   observable _____ .

3. A. H. Maslow's theory of human needs suggests that until
   survival and security needs are satisfied, man is actually
   _____ .

4. The *pressures* which move people toward need satisfaction
   are called _____ .

5. What happens after a need is satisfied?

ANSWERS

1. Physical and mental (pages 1 and 8)
2. Action, or behavior (page 13)
3. Insecure (page 15)
4. Drives (page 16)
5. Another need arises (page 26)

CHAPTER 2

MOTIVATION

All businesses have goals. Some of these might be short-range goals, such as increasing production rates. Others may be long-range goals, such as obtaining or exceeding a certain return on the money invested in the business.

People have short-range and long range goals also. A person's short-range goal might be to work well enough to obtain a raise. This will help fulfill the long-range goal of owning a home. It is safe to say that people are always goal-seeking. This being the case, you could safely say that:

1. The pressure to satisfy a need is the same as the pressure that moves us toward a goal. . . . . Page 49

2. A goal is established only after survival and security needs have been satisfied. . . . . Page 51

Your answer: 1. Bob was motivated to get a better job.

Apparently Bob was motivated to get a better job because when he got the job he changed his behavior. But isn't this just half the story?

Observe what Bob was doing.

Observe what made Bob quit doing it.

Make your decision on the basis of both observations.

Please return and try again.

Your answer: 2. Bob's promotion was the reward which ended his drive for a better job.

We don't think this is the best answer. It's true, but it's only half the story. If you observe what Bob did and then observe what happened to make him change his attitude, you will then see that two elements are involved, not just the one you selected.

Please consider the question again.

Your answer: 3. Both of these.

You are correct. Apparently Bob was unhappy because he felt he deserved a better position. In his drive for promotion he took out his feelings of dissatisfaction on his fellow employees.

It is by observing people's behavior that we can discover what is motivating and what is nonmotivating. Let's change Bob's case a little bit to advance this point.

Suppose that after getting the promotion, Bob continued to be a grouch. Which of the following statements do you think would express Bob's opinion of his promotion?

1. It's not the reward he was seeking . . . . .Page 52

2. It's nonmotivating . . . . .Page 55

3. It's motivating, anyway .Page 56

Your answer: 1. The pressure to satisfy a need is the same as the pressure that moves us toward a goal.

Good! You grasped the idea that there is a transfer of need satisfaction to goal satisfaction.

Anything that moves a person toward a goal is said to be motivating. If a pat on the back moves someone to try harder, then a pat on the back is motivating.

We said in the first chapter that Tom needed both transportation and recognition. These needs motivated him to buy an expensive car. Once he had the car, his needs were satisfied, and so he was no longer motivated toward that particular goal. He had his reward, and so was no longer driven to get the car.

As you can see from this, a man's needs motivate him to try for a certain goal, and the achievement of that goal ends that particular motivation.

Consider this example. Bob has been working very hard, even well after quitting time. His work is excellent, but his nerves seem to be getting pretty raw. This has been going on for weeks, and Bob has been getting pretty unpopular with his fellow workers. One day Bob's boss makes Bob his assistant. Bob continues to work hard, but his attitude changes from irritable to pleasant, and he becomes much easier to get along with.

Bob was irritable at one point but became pleasant again after being made assistant to the boss. Why?

1. Bob was motivated to get a better job . . . . Page 46

2. Bob's promotion was the reward which ended his drive for a better job. . . . . Page 47

3. Both of these . . . . Page 48

Your answer: 2. A goal is established only after survival and security needs have been satisfied.

No. What we are trying to demonstrate is the transfer of activity from need satisfaction to goal satisfaction. A man knows he needs a supply of water. He can carry water to his shelter everyday, but he is moved to obtain an easier supply of water. So he digs a well, thus achieving his goal and satisfying his need. He still has a need for an easy water supply and he has now gotten one, so the need to *get* one is reduced. Remember Tom, who had a need for recognition and so bought a very expensive car? In his case we can see that the ownership of the expensive car was his goal.

Please return and consider the other answer.

Your answer: 1. The promotion is not the reward Bob was seeking.

Excellent! A person is motivated to drive toward a particular goal, and the achievement of that goal is the reward that ends the drive. But the attitude Bob had after the promotion was the same as the attitude he had before, so it's a pretty safe bet that the promotion itself is not the reward Bob was seeking. Perhaps he wanted more responsibility with the promotion, or perhaps nothing about the job would ever satisfy him; we don't know.

Bob's situation shows us several things. For one, it shows that with a little careful observation we can usually find out what motivates people—not always, but usually. For another, it shows that the right rewards satisfy the need and end the drive, while the wrong rewards are dissatisfying and let the drive continue.

Of course, any number of different motivations exist in each person's life, and they may or may not be important. One man may be motivated to spend every waking hour studying and working at a particular business—because he wants to make a lot of money at it. Another man may be motivated to get out the car and drive downtown—because he wants a pizza. Some motivations seem particularly related to work, and from them we have selected a few that seem to be especially job-oriented. They are the motivations to:

> Be a thinker
> Avoid trouble
> Achieve
> Be liked

Over the next several pages we will consider these motives one at a time and show how they apply to job situations.

Suppose a person's dominant motive is to be a thinker. This motive might be expressed in more than one way. For instance, he might always want to be good at anything he tackles, or he might want to find satisfactory answers. His drive is to be reasonable, that is, to find a reasonable solution to most problems.

Ed was motivated to be a thinker. His drive was to figure out ways to improve things, and to be logical in his approach to everything.

However, Ed might possibly develop some off-beat solution to a problem which could conflict with the thinking of people around him. Here's an example:

The company Ed worked for produced radioactive materials for use in atomic energy piles. One of the big dangers in such a business is that of exposure to radiation. Ed, who is a research engineer working in a very "hot" area (one in which he is often exposed to radiation), takes the precautions necessary to protect himself against overexposure; in fact, he has been very carefully trained to do so.

Ed's boss knows that Ed is a thinker. Of the two possibilities mentioned below, which do you believe Ed's boss would be most concerned about?

1. Ed might *make a mistake* someday and not protect himself properly ....Page 57

2. Ed might *change his ideas* about the extent of the danger and get into serious trouble ....Page 58

Your answer: 2. It's nonmotivating.

Not exactly. Anything that moves a person toward *a goal* is motivating. In Bob's case, however, it appears that the promotion was not the reward he was after.

The promotion in itself was not a motivator in this case, because to be a motivator it must be a reward, and it would be a reward only if it satisfied some drive. If we assumed Bob was grouchy because he was motivated toward the goal of a better job, we were mistaken.

If a promotion were Bob's goal, even a promise of promotion might motivate him. In this case the promise becomes the motivator, and the promotion becomes the reward.

Please turn to page 52.

Your answer 3. It's motivating anyway.

You are missing the point. Anything that moves a person toward *a goal* is motivating, but the promotion was a satisfying
reward only if getting it was Bob's goal.

Please continue to page 52.

Your answer: 1. Ed might make a mistake someday and not protect himself properly.

Wel-l-l, maybe, but we think you could have selected a better answer. Everybody makes a mistake now and then, and it's nothing to be ashamed of. But to judge by what we know of Ed, it doesn't seem very likely that he'd make a mistake in this particular situation.

No, but he thinks a lot about his job, and it is entirely possible that he might decide for himself that the danger is not nearly as great as someone else has ruled that it is. *Then* he might overexpose himself to radiation—*not* through carelessness, but through having carefully and logically *made the wrong decision.*

Please proceed to page 58.

Your answer: 2. Ed might change his ideas about the extent of the danger and get into serious trouble.

This is the best answer. Consider the difference between what Ed knows and how he acts (here comes observation again). He *knows* that the working conditions are dangerous, but after looking the situation over and thinking about it for a period of time, he decides that it isn't as dangerous as he's been told. So he ignores some of the safety requirements and winds up in the hospital with a good dose of radiation sickness, maybe even some permanent damage.

If you have a man who is a thinker on a job that has a high danger potential, be constantly aware of his behavior, and remind him frequently of the danger to which he is exposed.

The second motivator we listed was the desire to avoid trouble, and by trouble we mean fear and anxiety. Take George, for example. The industry in which he is employed is noted for its ups and downs due to increases and decreases in business contracts. This creates budget and manpower problems, and large layoffs are not unusual. Sometimes it is necessary to lay off higher-income personnel in order to keep enough manpower for jobs that take less skill.

George has been a faithful employee for over 20 years. Because of raises or merit increases, he is making nearly as much money as a supervisor or leader. George is neither of these; he has been a good employee but he has never been offered a supervisor's job. Now his review comes up again and his supervisor calls him in for a talk. "George," says the supervisor, "you do fine work. I'm putting you in for another raise." George promptly replies:

1. "Thanks very much." . . . . Page 65

2. "Thanks, but no thanks!" . . . . Page 66

Your answer: 1. Job challenges.

Yes but. Yes—he likes to be challenged. But—would that be enough? There's more to satisfying an achiever than just giving him a challenging job.

Please return and consider the other answers.

Your answer: 2. Immediate feedback about his efforts.

Well, the achiever is quite anxious to know how well he achieves, but there is more involved in satisfying an achiever than immediate results. An achiever wants to be challenged and is willing to take risks, so he is anxious about the results of his efforts.

Please return and look over these answers again.

Your answer: 3. Risk taking.

An achiever will be willing to take risks, but this answer seems to us like you're just guessing. Or are you risk taking? If you had thoughtfully read this question, you could hardly have chosen this as the complete answer to what satisfies the achiever.

Please return and find a fuller understanding of the achievement motive.

Your answer: 4. All of these.

That's right! The achiever likes a challenging job, he wants to
know right now how he is doing, and he is willing to take
risks if there's a good chance they will give him the results he
needs to satisfy his need for achievement. It's rather
important, though, for you to remember to let the achievement-motivated person know how he's doing. Feedback on
the results he's getting will help keep him on the beam.

An achiever will constantly ask questions or make suggestions; he *wants* to do more than you require of him. And if
by chance you assigned him to a job without specific goals,
you'd probably be wasting his drive. (He might find such a
job quite frustrating, too.)

The last item on that little list we made was the motivation
to be liked. You may think, "Why make something special
out of that? Everybody wants to be liked." Well, it is true

that just about everybody does want to be liked, but some people want other things more; they may need to be thinkers or achievers or something else so badly that they will respond to those needs before any others.

We are talking now about the person whose need to be liked is greater than his other needs. He wants to avoid criticism or controversy; he doesn't like to take sides.

Do you remember Mary in Chapter 1? Her job performance didn't measure up to her actual ability because performance was not her strongest motivation. She preferred to be liked, and this motivated her to perform only at the level of those around her.

Now how about this case? Ray was a good engineer who worked for a west-coast company that manufactured a complex product. He was assigned to the eastern part of the country to generate sales and handle customer service, and he did quite a good job at taking care of customer complaints and problems. But his boss back home was never able to make out just what orders Ray sent back were the results of Ray's *sales* activities. This isn't much evidence, but it *is* enough to let us make some statement about Ray from those listed below.

1. Ray wanted to be liked . . . . Page 69

2. Ray lacked the skills for this assignment . . . . . Page 70

3. Both of the above . . . . Page 71

Your answer: 1. "Thanks very much."

Sure George says "Thanks." But he also turns down the raise. Believe it or not—he says "Thanks, but no thanks." George's goal is to retire, not to get into a salary bracket that competes with supervision. Furthermore, the last thing he wants is to compete on a wage level which may put him in a position to be laid off. He's playing it *safe*; he fears that he may lose his job if he makes *too* much money.

Please return and consider the other answer!

Your answer: 2. "Thanks, but no thanks."

Right. George has been around the company long enough to know what his safe salary level is. He knew that if he made more money he would be over his safe capacity to produce. Understanding himself and his situation, he wisely turned down the offer.

There actually can be times when offering a man more money can endanger his job because it puts him in a competitive position with others or in an income bracket high enough so that economic factors, rather than his own productivity, can affect his job. George is motivated to avoid fear and anxiety, so he turns down anything that would make him have to prove himself beyond his comfortable abilities to do so. This particular motivation, to avoid fear and anxiety (trouble) is a very strong one; it is a form of the most basic of all motivations—the need to survive.

While we are dealing with this motivation, that of avoiding trouble, we might point out that most people will tend to agree with your suggestions and decisions. After all, you're the supervisor, aren't you? So why look for trouble by bumping heads with the supervisor? This being the case, you will have to think up ways to get ideas from people, not just agreement.

One technique that would help would be to avoid making too positive statements. For instance, if you say, "This section is supposed to turn out 100 blivvet parts an hour. You guys better hop to it," all you're going to get (to your face) is "Yessir." No help, no suggestions, just "Yessir." So try a different approach; something like "We've been planning on 100 blivvet parts an hour from this section, but we can't quite seem to make it. Let's all talk the problem over and see if we can come up with some ideas that will get the section up to that rate."

You may think that this is sugaring the men up when you'd rather give them a chewing out, but one of your needs is for achievement, (or you wouldn't be in your job), and this technique works. It works because you are doing things that motivate people; you are: (1) showing confidence in your men, (2) asking them to deal with a problem instead of a person (you), (3) opening the door to two-way communication between yourself and the men of the section, and (4) involving them in the making of decisions, which increases their personal commitment.

You may know from your own experience that the *achievement motive* is one of the strongest motives of all. Few people tackle a job without wanting to master it and go on to something tougher. A person driven by the achievement motive does not like failure at all; he needs success. (Achievement is the third item on that brief list of job motivations we made awhile ago).

To better understand the achievement motive, consider the list below, and choose which item best describes what the achievement-motivated person wants.

Your answer: 1. Ray wanted to be liked.

Wrong! We all want to be liked; we've
mentioned that. But Ray did not perform
on this basis. Nothing in the brief case
history would indicate this. Did you conclude that the customer probably liked Ray
because he took care of their problems so
well? This could very well be. But Ray did
his job according to his ability. He was a
good engineer, and when the customer had
a problem, he responded to it. That does
not indicate any unusual motivation to be
liked. Ray happened to be a pleasant guy,
but he could have been a real grouch and
still have been a first-rate trouble shooter.

Please return and try for a better answer.

Your answer: 2. Ray lacked the skills for this assignment.

You are correct. Actually, Ray's case had nothing at all to do with motives; it was concerned with abilities, and while Ray was a good engineer, he was not a good salesman.

The desire to be liked does not necessarily mean that a person so motivated will act contrary to the company's goals. Mary did, of course, when she cut production so her fellow workers would like her. But if it had been more important to her to have someone in authority like her, she might have kept her production up, which would have fitted in quite nicely with one of the company's goals—high production.

You see, it's not really safe to judge motives. It's easy to evaluate drives as good or bad—but it's also a mistake. It's not the drives but the way they are handled that makes them good or bad. People are people and they all have drives, and as supervisors we do well to guide people as they are, not as we would have them be.

We hope that by this time you are getting some feel for people's needs and motivations in job situations. To get on with it, now, please complete the following statement with one of the words given below: Anything that _____ us toward a goal is motivating.

1. moves . . . . Page 72

2. helps . . . . Page 73

Your answer: 3. Both of the above.

Why? From the evidence, Ray wasn't much of a salesman. But nothing in the case history would indicate that he was performing in response to his desire to be liked. Did you conclude that the customers probably liked Ray because he took care of their problems so well? This could very well be. But Ray did his job according to his ability. He was a good engineer and when the customer had a problem, he responded to it, that's all.

Please return and try for a better answer.

Your answer: 1. Moves.

You are correct. Anything that *moves* us toward a goal is motivating.

Suppose you were hiking and after a while became very thirsty. You went in search of a stream you knew was in the vicinity, even though it meant leaving the trail. You found water, sure enough. After a good, long drink, you returned to the trail and continued on your hike.

The *need* for water was motivating. What ended the need?

1. Finding the stream . . . . Page 74

2. The good, long drink . . . . Page 75

Your answer: 2. Helps.

No. Our definition is "Anything that *moves* us toward a goal is motivating."

Please turn to page 72.

Your answer: 1. Finding the stream.

Of course you were glad to find the stream, but you were still thirsty.

Finding the stream didn't satisfy your thirst. It was only after the good, long drink that your need for water ended and you returned to your former activity—hiking the trail.

Motivation has two basic elements: (1) the drives that move us toward goals and (2) the rewards that end the drive. Your thirst drove you to look for water, and drinking ended your thirst.

Please continue to page 75.

Your answer: 2. The good, long drink.

Right. Motivation has two basic elements: (1) the drives that move us toward goals and (2) the rewards that end the drive. Your thirst drove you to look for water, and drinking ended your thirst.

Which of the following is probably more true when a person is motivated by the desire to achieve, he needs:

1. Immediate feedback about the results of his work. Page 76

2. Long-range goals that do not depend on immediate knowledge of results . . . . Page 78

Your answer: 1. Immediate feedback about the results of his work.

Right. Some people like to get feedback about how they are doing because this helps keep them in line with the long-range goals toward which they are working. But whether or not feedback is necessary as a guide toward a goal, the achiever must have feedback merely for the satisfaction of his drive—his need to know that he is achieving.

Here are some key associations that may help you remember something about motives:

Motive	Behavior
To be liked	Avoids conflict
To be a thinker	Favors logical approaches
To avoid trouble	Plays it safe
To achieve	Wants to excel

Whether it was easy or difficult to get to this point, you probably now have a pretty good grasp of the subject. Now please proceed to page 79.

Your answer: 2. Long-range goals, that do not depend on immediate knowledge of results.

Not true about the person motivated by achievement.

The achiever needs feedback about how he is doing all along the line. Achievers can work toward long-range goals but some feedback on how they are doing is needed to keep the individual well motivated. Other people, with other motivating drives, can set long-range goals but not getting feedback does not upset them. This is a big distinction.

Please continue to page 76.

Complete this brief test and then turn to the next page to check your answers. If you miss any of these questions, you can review the subject by going back to the pages indicated after the answers.

1. Anything that moves a person toward a goal is said to be

   _____ .

2. Some situations can be motivating, others nonmotivating. How can we tell whether or not a person is motivated?

3. Motivation has two parts. Can you name them?

4. Can a person be motivated to avoid trouble?

5. What do we call the motive that causes a person to like challenges, to take risks, and to want feedback about how he is doing?

ANSWERS

1. Motivating (page 49)

2. By observing the person's behavior (page 48)

3. Drives and rewards. Drives which cause a person to act and rewards which terminate or end the drive. (page 49)

4. Yes (page 58)

5. Achievement motive   (page 68)

CHAPTER 3

GOALS, MOTIVATIONS, AND ATTITUDES

When we accept the fact that an individual has needs which must be satisfied, we can easily understand that he sets goals for himself which satisfy those needs when the goals are obtained.

While man has learned that it is rewarding to reach one's goal, he has also learned that some goals can be attained only against the drive of a much stronger motivation, and that these goals should be avoided.

Take Dave's case, for example. He operated a machine on which the material to be shaped was hand-fed and hand-removed. As a safety measure, the machine was designed with two START buttons, positioned about three feet apart, that had to be pushed at the same time in order to operate the machine. This prevented the operator from accidentally having one hand in the machine when it started its cycle. The extra motion involved in this two-hand operation made the day's production per machine just a little less than it would have been with one-hand operation, but safety saves money, and the company was satisfied to put safety first.

Well, Dave had several motivations (most people do); he wanted recognition, he wanted to achieve, and he wanted to make more money. He found that by jamming one of the START buttons on, he could feed the machine with one hand, operate it with the other, and turn out a little higher production. He was also a bit of a thinker, and had decided for himself that the danger of losing a hand was greatly overrated.

Dave had a couple of close calls but he got away with his system for almost three days before the foreman saw what he was doing. Then he suddenly found himself in the foreman's office, facing the foreman and the shop steward, and catching a double-barreled blast for what he'd been doing.

You see, the foreman had the very strong drive, which the shop steward was quite willing to support, to keep his men safe and free from injury. And Dave found that it might not be worthwhile to try to reach his goals in *that* particular way against that particular drive.

Now, we know that removal of need satisfaction does not remove the need. Dave still needed to achieve a higher level of production and he still needed to make more money (though maybe he didn't need recognition as much as before). What do you think he did after being caught violating such an important safety regulation?

1. He observed proper safety procedures, and tried to raise his production legitimately, by developing
   greater skill. . . . . Page 83

2. He kept on gimmicking the START button, being more careful not to let the foreman see him . . . . . . Page 84

Your answer: 1. He observed proper safety procedures, and tried to raise his production legitimately, by developing greater skill.

This could be right. He had gotten quite a going over, and he knew that he risked trouble with both the company and the union if he kept on doing what he'd done. The possibility of losing his insurance coverage or compensation in case of an accident didn't bother him at all; you remember that he had decided that the chance of his getting hurt was greatly overrated. But fear of the other trouble he could get into might very well be stronger than his need for achievement or more money.

Please proceed to page 85.

Your answer: 2. He kept on gimmicking the START button, being more careful not to let the foreman see him.

This could be right. He'd gotten quite a going over, and he knew that he risked trouble with both the company and the union if he kept on doing what he'd done. But the need to achieve—and to make more money—could very well outweigh his fear of trouble. Of course, the possibility of losing his insurance coverage or compensation in case of an accident didn't bother him at all, because he had already decided that the chance of his getting hurt was practically zero. Like many, he felt that accidents only happen to the other guy. So if his needs were stronger than his fears, he would keep on with his dangerous practice until stopped.

Please proceed to page 85.

(from page 83 or 84)   85

We saw that the answer to the last question depended on whether Dave wanted most to satisfy certain needs or avoid punishment.

The urge to seek and achieve a goal is a basic one, but we also like to avoid punishment whenever possible. From infancy on, we learn to seek rewards by doing the right thing and to avoid punishment by *not* doing the *wrong* thing.

We would find it very much easier than it is to understand a person's behavior if we could only measure the strength of his drive, how rewarding the goal would be to him, and how *un*rewarding he would find it to be punished.

A word of caution: Except in extreme and unusual cases, avoidance of punishment will not move a person toward a goal unless that goal happens to be one the person wants to reach. That is why it is almost always a mistake, and sometimes a very serious one, to use punishment as a means of motivating a person toward a goal he doesn't want to reach.

Punishment can be used to block someone from a goal they want to reach. If the fear of punishment is greater than the desire to reach a goal, the goal will be given up; if the desire to reach a goal is greater than the fear of punishment, the goal will be reached in spite of the punishment. Whether or not Dave will continue to bypass the safety arrangement on his machine will depend on whether he wants to reach his goals of achievement and more money more than he fears the punishment he'll get if he's caught again.

In Dave's case, the fear of punishment was used for Dave's own welfare; to help preserve his physical safety. Often, though, the use of punishment presents some tough ethical problems—it may work, but is it right? Think it over.

As we have said, we all tend to seek rewards and avoid punishment. We can easily understand, therefore, that any individual will bring to his job certain attitudes and behaviors based on what he expects to do about his goals.

Before we talk about this, please answer the following question: Do you believe that most people

1. want to do good work . . . . Page 87

   or that they

2. work just enough to get by? . . . . Page 88

Your answer: 1. Most people want to do good work.

Yes, this is the right answer. In the early days of industry, managers assumed that a worker did not want to work, that he had to be started and kept running, just like a machine, and that anything that achieved this was acceptable.

It has been only in recent years that management has recognized workers as individuals, not machines. When a worker is doing just enough to get by, today's supervisor tries to find out why.

Please proceed to page 89.

Your answer: 2. Most people work just enough to get by.

We do not believe this is so. Whenever we observe a worker doing just enough to get by we suspect that something is missing from the job situation.

It used to be that management thought of men on the job as so many machines. Like machines, they had to be started and kept running, and anything that achieved this was acceptable.

Today's supervisor tries to recognize that the worker is an individual with needs and goals, and that he will move to satisfy his goals unless he is blocked from obtaining them.

Please proceed to page 89.

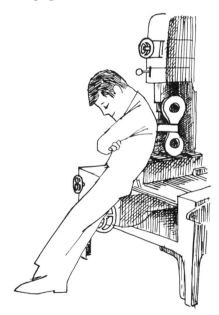

It is very important that you understand that people are much more than just machines; they bring to the job their individual purposes and goals and they expect satisfaction from their work. That satisfaction is not the same for all people, but it *is* job-connected. When a worker is performing below par or at the minimum acceptable level, something about the job or about him needs a closer look.

Back in 1939 a study of morale factors was made. A list of these factors was set up and given to a group of workers to rank in order of importance to them. Which of the following rankings would you say was favored by the majority of these workers.

1. Understanding, counsel on personal feelings, promotion on merit ....Page 94

2. Fair pay, job security, interesting work ....Page 95

3. Credit for work done, interesting work, fair pay ..Page 96

Your answer: 1. Satisfied.

This is a good answer, but it's not the best. Let's say that all the members of a group get a 7% raise except Ben, who gets a 5% raise. A raise should be quite a satisfaction; that is, it should be what we call a satisfier. But Ben's raise is not as much as the others in his group got, so he is dissatisfied; the raise is actually a dissatisfier.

Or let's say that Ben is promoted to a management level and is given an office which is smaller than that occupied by another man on the same level. The office, which should have been a satisfier, becomes a dissatisfier because Ben thinks it isn't good enough.

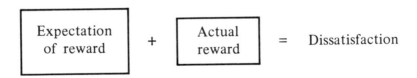

If it is not up to our expectations, a reward can be a dissatisfier.

Please return and try to select a more complete answer.

Your answer: 2. Dissatisfied.

A good answer, but not the best. If a raise, for example, were
not what a worker expected, he would be dissatisfied; that is,
the raise would be what we call a dissatisfier. But if the raise
was as much as the worker expected, it would be a satisfier.

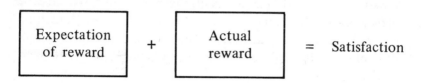

You see, whether something is a satisfier or a dissatisfier
depends on what was expected.

Please return and select a more complete answer.

Your answer: 3. Both satisfied and dissatisfied.

Right. A person who gets a raise, for example, may be both satisfied and dissatisfied about it—satisfied because he got a raise and dissatisfied because it wasn't bigger. We could say in such a case that the raise is both a satisfier and a dissatisfier.

A man can have the same reactions regarding his needs for recognition, achievement, or what have you. Even though he may not be able to pinpoint just what his needs are, he will probably be able to tell when they have been satisfied—and when they haven't.

Because of his needs, every man has a drive toward some goal or other. When that goal-seeking drive runs into an obstacle between the man and his goal, as in the sketch below, what do you suppose the man's behavior would show?

1. Frustration . . . . .Page 98

2. Contentment . . . . .Page 100

Your answer: 4. I don't understand.

Well, let's look at it this way. Suppose a group of workers got a 7% raise across the board. It's what they had expected and so they are satisfied; the raise is what we call a satisfier. Now, suppose they expected 7% but only got 4%. Would they be satisfied? You bet they wouldn't! Such a raise, even though it's more money, would not satisfy, and so it is what we would call a dissatisfier.

You see, whether something is a satisfier or a dissatisfier depends on what is expected.

Please return and select the best answer.

Your answer: 1. Understanding, counsel on personal feelings, promotion on merit.

This ranking could be tops for a lot of people at one time or another, but it was not found to be the most important ranking in this study. Most of the workers, most of the time, did not choose these factors as most important.

Please return and make another selection.

Your answer: 2. Fair pay, job security, interesting work.

Not the ones chosen in this study!

We suspect this ranking would be the top choice of persons working at a safe level of performance. However, it was not the ranking these workers felt was most important to most of them most of the time.

Please return and select another ranking.

Your answer: 3. Credit for work done, interesting work, and fair pay.

Yes, these were the most important morale factors to most of the workers most of the time. It is quite interesting to notice that they placed credit for work done and interesting work ahead of fair pay and job security. As a matter of fact, they ranked job security last!

In 1964, a study conducted by F. Herzberg, B. Housner, and B. Snyderman* showed that a group of engineers ranked a list of job attitude factors in this order:

1. Achievement   4. Responsibility
2. Recognition   5. Advancement
3. Work itself   6. Salary

This study compared with the one made in 1939, 25 years before, indicates that people haven't changed much in what they consider most important about a job.

As you know, anything that makes a person move toward a goal can be considered motivation. On the job we try to get and keep people moving toward the company's goals, and doing this is one of the hardest jobs facing a supervisor.

In tackling the problem of motivating people, let us first examine what a person expects from a job. He expects to be paid about what others are paid for the same type of work he is doing; he expects decent working conditions; and he expects to have friendly relationships with others.

---

*Herzberg, Frederick, *et al.*, *The Motivation to Work,* John Wiley and Sons, New York (1964).

Now, depending on the degree to which a person is able to fulfill his expectations, he may be:

Your answer: 1. Frustration.

Right. We assume that a person wants to do good work. When something blocks him from achieving this goal, his actions (his behavior) will show it.

Some of the ways a person may behave when some barrier keeps him from doing his best work are listed below:

1. He does just enough to get by.

2. He grumbles about "company policy."

3. He's often late to work.

4. He abuses his privileges, such as long lunches, sick leaves, and other benefits.

5. He makes more than his share of mistakes.

6. He constantly gets into gripe sessions with other employees.

A person can be motivated in several ways, a few of which are: the removal of barriers that stand between him and whatever it is he expects from his job, knowing that his immediate superiors understand the needs that drive him to seek a particular goal, and by becoming involved in decisions.

Our next chapter will go into greater detail about barriers and how individuals react to certain situations created by them. Before going on to this subject, however, we would like to test your understanding of goals, motivation, and attitudes.

Which of the following statements about goal-oriented behavior is true?

Your answer: 2. Contentment.

Let's suppose that you operate a lathe, and that your goal is to do a good job of it. The foreman has assigned a particular job to you, and you've drawn the necessary materials from the storeroom and started your setup. Then you discover that the blueprint is so badly smudged that you can hardly read it, and so your setup time runs almost twice as long as usual.

The dirty blueprint is a barrier between you and your goal, and we suspect that you would be at least a little dissatisfied with the way things were running. If the same thing happened on the next job, and the next, would your behavior show that you were contented?

Please return and choose another answer.

Your answer: 1. People learn to seek and avoid goals, depending on conditions.

Not so.

What we said earlier was that people learn to *seek goals* and *avoid punishment.* As people grow older, experience seems to strengthen this tendency.

Please continue to page 102.

Your answer: 2. People learn to seek goals and avoid punishment.

That is correct. Of course, tastes differ, and there are times when a reward to one man might seem like punishment to another. But that's beside the point; we all tend to seek rewards and avoid punishment.

We have already said that certain aspects of a job, such as job security, interesting work, and credit for work done could raise or lower a person's morale. We also said that, depending on the situation, these factors could be:

1. Satisfiers or dissatisfiers . . . . .Page 103

2. Things that should be sought or avoided . . . . . . Page 104

Your answer: 1. Satisfiers or Dissatisfiers.

That is correct. It is desirable that the workers find motiva-
tional impulses from the job situation. Motivated workers do
better than average work, are satisfied with their jobs, and
identify their goals with the company's goals. When examining the factors which contribute to motivation, we first
look at:

1. What we expect of the worker . . . . .Page 105

2. What the worker expects of the job . . . . .Page 106

Your answer: 2. Things that should be sought or avoided.

No. You must be confusing job morale factors with goal-seeking attitudes.

Remember our discussion about morale factors; recall that one group of workers ranked credit for work done as most important, while another group said achievement was most rewarding? Then we discussed the fact that these things could be either satisfiers or dissatisfiers depending on the situation.

Please turn to page 103.

Your answer: 1. What we expect of the worker.

No. We think it is more important to learn what the worker expects of the job. Once you have some feel for the expectations a person brings to the job you are in a better position to know what to expect from him.

Please proceed to page 106.

Your answer: 2. What the worker expects of the job.

Yes, this is correct.

Once you have some feel for the expectations a person brings to the job you are in a better position to know what to expect from him.

Now, one final question. The worker's behavior is an indication of whether or not he is motivated to do good work. When a person's behavior tells you he is dissatisfied, what should you start looking for?

1. A good reason to fire him . . . . .Page 107

2. The barrier that's blocking his
    good performance . . . . .Page 108

Your answer: 1. A good reason to fire him.

No. This is a last resort.

Dr. Robert Blake, coauthor of *The Managerial Grid,** would probably classify you as a 9−1, person, which means you have a high concern for production and a low concern for people. Very often these are not compatible factors.

When a person expresses dissatisfaction it is probably because something stands between him and his best job performance. Why not find the cause of this behavior and try to take corrective action? And don't be surprised if you find less cause to worry about production.

Please continue to page 108.

---

*Blake, R.R., and Jane S. Mouton, *The Managerial Grid,* Gulf Publishing Company, Houston (1964).

Your answer: 2. The barrier that's blocking his good performance.

Good. We can't overemphasize the importance of finding the reasons behind people's unsatisfactory behavior or performance. Finding the barrier is the subject of our next chapter.

Please proceed to page 109.

Complete this brief test and then turn to the next page to check your answers. If you miss any of these questions, you can review the subject by going back to the pages indicated after the answers.

1. Does man *learn* that a goal is rewarding or does he know it *instinctively?*

2. Man seeks _____ and avoids _____ .

3. People approach their job with certain expectations. If the job meets their expectations they are usually satisfied. What is a person's attitude when the job does not meet his expectations?

4. When something blocks a person from a goal, the person becomes_____ .

5. Examine the following list:

   Achievement   Work itself
   Responsibility   Salary
   Advancement   Recognition

Which of these would you say were factors affecting a worker's attitude about his job?

ANSWERS

1. He *learns* that a goal is rewarding (page 81)

2. Goals, punishment (page 85)

3. They are usually dissatisfied (page 92)

4. Frustrated (page 98)

5. All of them (page 96)

CHAPTER 4

ELIMINATING BARRIERS
TO PRODUCTIVE WORK

You might say that this is where the story really begins. When you realize that all people have needs to satisfy and that they are driven by goal-seeking motives, you can improve the environment in which they work.

There's no denying that it would be nice if all employees were hard-working, productive, and contented. That simply is not the case, of course, but why make matters worse by ignoring needs that aren't being met and goals that aren't being reached; that just leads to frustration for everybody.

We must recognize the fact that sources of discontent are never-ending, and that people will never be able to work in a continuously happy state, no matter how much they may want to. There will always be barriers for people to overcome before they can reach their goals, and this can cause great frustration. But when people's expectations are fairly met, they are contented and operate at a more productive level. A major part of your duty is to look for and help overcome those barriers; that is a mark of good supervision.

Now, just what do we mean by "barriers?"

1. Things that keep a worker from
   doing a good job . . . . Page 116

2. Things that are dissatisfiers . . . . Page 119

3. I don't know . . . . Page 120

111

Your answer: 1. Approach-approach.

That is correct. Jack had to make a choice between two desirable goals, and the two desires conflicted.

Barriers cause conflict because they require decisions; somebody has to decide what to do about them. And, as shown here, it isn't always a case of just choosing the better of two alternatives, but of selecting the best out of several.

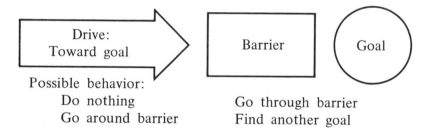

Drive:
Toward goal

Barrier

Goal

Possible behavior:
   Do nothing   Go through barrier
   Go around barrier Find another goal

What makes things worse in this figure (and in many actual situations) is that none of the alternatives is particularly good; none of them *removes* the barrier.

Try an example: Your company has won a big military contract. You estimate that your part of the work will take X dollars, but you're allowed only half that. This is a real barrier to satisfactory performance of your job. What are the alternatives?

If you do nothing, there is a strong possibility that the company will be heavily penalized for default or for missing its promised delivery date.

If you try to go around the barrier by compromising the quality of the product, it won't hold up in the field and there will be all kinds of trouble.

If you try to go through the barrier by overdrawing the budget allotted to you, your abilities as a manager will be questioned, and you might get pulled off the job. This would neither help you nor solve the problem.

If you choose another goal (such as looking for another job, perhaps), that may get you out from under but it still doesn't solve the problem.

The only good solution is to *remove* the barrier, and the best way to do that might be to request a budget review. You may not get all you originally asked for, but you may get more than the company originally allowed you.

Now, insufficient budget is a *big* barrier to good job performance, but there are lots of little things that are just as surely barriers that will keep a man from doing the job as well as he should (and would like to).

Which of the three lists given below would you say presents barriers to good job performance?

1. Inadequate salary, poor working conditions, no cigarette or candy machines . . . . Page 121

2. Poor instructions, not enough time allocated, nobody listening to work problems . . . . Page 122

3. No benefit program, poor personnel counseling, not enough paid holidays . . . . Page 125

Your answer: 2. Approach-avoidance.

No. This can't be the right answer because Jack's conflict was not caused by anything he was trying to avoid. He looked forward to both meetings. The conflict was in deciding which meeting to attend.

Please return and try again.

Your answer: 3. Avoidance-avoidance.

No. You might have made this selection because you felt Jack had to avoid or miss one meeting. But Jack wasn't trying to avoid either meeting. His problem was to make a choice between two desirable things.

Please return and try again.

Your answer: 1. Barriers are things that keep a worker from doing a good job.

That is correct. Barriers can be very frustrating, because whenever we come up against one, we have to make a choice, and whenever we have to make a choice, we have the possibility of a conflict. In some cases the conflict doesn't amount to much at all, but in other cases it can upset a man's whole life.

Psychologists say that when we are faced with a decision, that is, when we have to choose between two goals, we have to take one of three different courses of action, any of which will result in conflict. We may want to approach both goals, we may want to approach one goal and avoid the other, or we may want to avoid both goals. We might diagram the problem this way:

This choice	Creates this behavior	With this result
Between two desirable goals	Approach-approach	Conflict
Between a desirable goal and an undesirable goal	Approach-avoidance	Conflict
Between two undesirable goals	Avoidance-avoidance	Conflict

We can show examples of each of these types of behavior. Do you remember Mary, who cut down her production rate so she wouldn't get ahead of the women she worked with? She had an *approach-approach* conflict; she had to choose between two desirable goals. Mary wanted to do a good job (as we have decided most people do) but she wanted also to be liked, so she chose to do less than her best in order to be popular.

Dave's case illustrates the *approach-avoidance* conflict. He had a desirable goal—that of making more money, and an undesirable goal—the punishment he might receive if he were found jamming the safety switch on his machine.

For an example of an *avoidance-avoidance* conflict we can imagine a man who is working at a job he doesn't particularly like and paying for a house he doesn't care much for, either. Losing his job would be an undesirable goal because he needs the money to pay for the house, among other things. And losing the house would be an undesirable goal because he can't afford to get another one at this time.

(from page 117)

Let's examine a new situation and see what type of conflict it presents. Jack has an appointment for this afternoon with one of his company's best customers, and he has just been notified that there will be a special and urgent meeting of all vice presidents at that time. Jack wants very much to keep both of these appointments, but obviously he is going to have to choose between them. What type of conflict does this represent?

1. Approach-approach . . . . Page 112

2. Approach-avoidance . . . . Page 114

3. Avoidance-avoidance . . . . Page 115

Your answer: 2. Barriers are things that are dissatisfiers.

That is incorrect. When we mentioned satisfiers and dissatisfiers we said that a satisfier—for instance a raise—could in certain situations be a dissatisfier. We pointed out that any one thing could satisfy or dissatisfy. The determining factor was whether or not it came up to our expectations.

A barrier is a barrier, a hindrance to an individual trying to do his job. Certainly, not doing a good job leaves a person unsatisfied, but to identify a barrier as a dissatisfier is to miss the basic point, and that is that a barrier is something that prevents a worker from doing a good job.

Now return and select the right answer.

Your answer: 3. I don't know.

Perhaps this sketch will make it more clear to you:

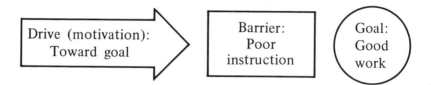

This worker is motivated by a desire to perform; his goal is to do good work. He will have trouble reaching that goal, however, because of the fact that he has had poor instruction.

Anything getting between the worker and his goal becomes a barrier.

Now return and select the right answer.

Your answer: 1. Inadequate salary, poor working conditions, no cigarette or candy machines.

This is not a good choice. Inadequate salary and no cigarette or candy machines could be dissatisfiers, but they don't get directly between the worker and his job as real barriers do. Even poor working conditions are hardly ever barriers to the worker who really wants to do a good job. (We'll mention that again later on).

Please return and try to do better.

Your answer: 2. Poor instructions, not enough hours allocated, nobody listening to problems.

This is the correct choice; these are the types of barriers that can keep a worker from reaching a high level of performance.

We have said that barriers produce conflict because they require a person to make a choice between two or more alternatives. But what happens when none of the alternatives is satisfactory—when none of them solves the problem?

Well, then the person faced with the conflict becomes frustrated, and frustration can be quite painful mentally. When you *must* solve a problem and *can't*, you can be pretty uncomfortable. It's only natural for a person to try to protect himself in such a case, to try to avoid the pain of frustration. Therefore he may do one of the following:

1. Change his goals, which just leaves the problem unsolved.

2. Persuade himself that the barrier isn't really there, which will just cause more frustration as he continues to beat against it.

3. Quit trying to solve the problem, which, of course, leaves it unsolved.

4. Become aggressive and bull his way through the barrier no matter what the cost, which could cost a great deal indeed.

In your position you should try to be sensitive to people's behavior, and be aware when that behavior indicates that some barrier is keeping them from the job performance you have a right to expect from them. As a matter of fact, you might find it useful to make behavior the barometer that tells you when a person is having trouble with a barrier, so that you may give it your attention.

One type of barrier to good performance (and one that's seldom mentioned by the employee) is fear or anxiety. Everybody has at least a little fear or anxiety about something, whether they know it or not. In a work situation it could be fear of getting fired a few years before retirement, or that the company is going broke and will have to reduce its work force. Or it might even be something that is actually good; promotion to a higher position or transfer to a new situation may cause a great deal of fear or anxiety if the person concerned lacks confidence in his ability to handle the new situation.

A word of caution: Every worker's job performance is affected to some extent by his personal life. If your organization offers personnel counseling, and if you think that one of your workers should take advantage of such service, recommend that he do so and stop there. No supervisor should ever allow himself knowingly to become involved in a worker's personal life.

Now, when you recognize that some barrier may be keeping one of your men from his best job performance, what should you do?

1. Sit tight and hope the problem disappears . . . Page 126

2. Call the man into your office and lay down the law. After all, he has obligations to the company just as the company has obligations to him . . . . Page 127

3. Have an informal discussion with the man to try to compare viewpoints . . . . Page 128

Your answer: 3. No benefit program, poor personnel counseling, not enough paid holidays.

Of course you're just fooling around, now, to see what would be said about this answer. None of these items is apt to stand directly between the worker and the work he is trying to do.

Please return and try again.

Your answer: 1. Sit tight and hope the problem disappears.

This is a popular solution—but it's not a good one. Some supervisors do just this, sweep the problem under the rug and try to forget it, but it isn't at all the best thing to do. It is possible for a frustrated or disappointed person to find his own solution to his problems, but, unfortunately, what so often happens is that the individual changes his goal or, even more simply, gives up. Performance gets even worse.

In a nut shell, he who sits tight and hopes the problem will disappear usually winds up with a bigger problem.

Please return and try again.

Your answer: 2. Call the man into your office and lay down the law.

No. This kind of discipline can increase a person's frustration. You might actually drive him into a do-nothing shell, as it were, where his attitudes and desires could work in opposition to your goals.

It is better to try to find out what stands between people and a good performance. Laying down the law might give *you* temporary satisfaction, but it won't solve the problem.

Please return and try to select the right answer.

Your answer: 3. Have an informal discussion with the man to try to compare viewpoints.

That's right. When a man doesn't deliver the required level of performance, or when his behavior indicates that something is wrong, it's time for a talk. And when that time comes, you should try to do the following:

1. Find the barrier or barriers keeping the man from the proper level of performance.

2. If you sense conflict, get it out in the open.

3. Listen to the man! Even when they try to, people often do not say what they mean. You will have to make an effort to get the meaning behind the words.

4. Make sure that both you and the man you're talking to have the same goals. He might have goals that don't match yours and the company's.

Let's illustrate these points with examples. Ernie is an eager worker but his work has a higher rejection rate than the company can tolerate. Also, you have noticed that Ernie sometimes gets extremely frustrated when an assembly isn't going right for him. Something obviously stands between Ernie and the minimum acceptable performance and you finally decide that:

1. Ernie is too eager. He's so concerned about doing a good job that his anxiousness acts as a barrier, causing him to make mistakes . . . . Page 134

2. Ernie lacks the necessary skills for the job . . . . Page 135

Your answer: 1. Suggest he buckle down and start doing his work.

Not the best action. Pete may say "O.K." and actually start preparing a report, but you haven't gotten to the bottom of the problem. Chances are he will drift back to his original behavior.

You must determine what is keeping Pete from following your instructions.

Please return and try again.

Your answer: 2. Find out what's bugging him.

Certainly, get it out into the open.

You may discover that Pete simply cannot accept your goals or guidelines. If that's the case, the sooner you find it out, the better. In any event, talking the situation over with Pete gives you a chance to apply yourself directly to his problem, whereas taking other alternatives only reinforces his attitude. And that, of course, could affect the performance of the whole group.

When you talk with men like Pete, remember that you want to find out what their goals are and then establish your own. You might even go along toward Pete's goals a little way before you try to bring him around to your viewpoint. This would show that you were interested in what Pete had to offer and might well be a help in finding out what his goals are. What's more, it might help you discover a way of achieving both goals with little or no sacrifice on either side.

If Pete could not be persuaded to budge from his position, you would have to (1) transfer him, (2) dismiss him, or (3) compromise with him. Of course, you could (4) do nothing, but since it would not improve the performance of the group, you don't even consider it.

Actually, the situation itself often suggests which is the most suitable action. However, you do not give yourself a chance to choose the best alternative unless you consider them all carefully.

Now let's turn our attention to listening as a means of uncovering barriers. This means that you must pay close attention to what is said, but it also means that people must be allowed to talk things out. The more you hear, the more clues you will have about what is interfering with performance. This is particularly true of gripes; never dismiss gripes as unimportant. It is possible that they are unimportant, but it is probable that they contain valuable information.

Let's use this example. Joe operates a machine that reproduces blueprints; his output is the lowest in the group, well below the average. You call him in to ask him why he isn't getting out more prints. You're a good listener, so you *don't* say, "Joe, you aren't putting out the work. This is your first warning—you'll have to improve or I'll have to replace you." No, you don't say anything like that, because all you will have to listen to will be, "Yes sir, I'll do my best."

Instead, you say something like, "Joe, you aren't putting out the work, so I figure you must have some kind of a problem. Anything I can do to help?" Then you'll get something to listen to, such as, "Well, look, in the first place, people are always interrupting me to ask for service. And there's that machine I'm assigned to; it's been around here since Washington was president; I have a helluva time feeding paper into it. If we had some decent equipment, there'd be no problem."

If you listened closely, you found a lot of information in that gripe. What clues has Joe given you about the problem?

Your answer: 3. Tell him that if he continues to ignore your instructions he'll be either transferred or dismissed.

No. At times threatening people will get them to perform, but not at their top level. What's more, this approach does nothing toward removing barriers, and you need to know the reasons why Pete is behaving as he is.

Please return and try again.

Your answer: 1. Ernie is too eager.

No, that's not the answer. Eagerness in itself is not a barrier to satisfactory performance. An eager worker who finds himself making mistakes by working too fast will correct this problem on his own. Eagerness is to be encouraged. If we thought eagerness was Ernie's barrier we would figure out some way to dampen it, but the chances are that this would not make any difference.

Please return and choose the other answer.

Your answer: 2. Ernie lacks the necessary skills for the job.

That's it. You knew that eagerness is seldom a barrier to performance, so you looked for another cause. Lack of skill is a very real barrier to performance. In this case you should explain to Ernie, without being rough on him, that he just doesn't have the skills for the job. Immediately that's done you should find out just what his goals are, so you can help him find a way to reach them.

Ernie will probably tell you that his goal is to do a bang-up job. You have observed his eagerness and of course you'd like him to be able to reach that goal. Quite possibly the right answer would be for Ernie to get some training to bring his job skill up to satisfactory standards.

Let's take another case of conflict. We'll assume that your group is responsible for job-improvement studies. You have set certain goals for the group and have laid down guidelines for their achievement, and you expect the work effort to produce studies which follow the patterns suggested by those guidelines. Everyone in the group applies himself to the task except Pete, who is senior man in the group and next in line for your job. He spends his time contacting other groups to discuss his approach to the job and criticize the studies prepared by others. Pete's behavior indicates that his is in direct conflict with your goals and expectations. When you decide it's time to talk with him, which of the following do you do?

1. Suggest he buckle down and start doing his work Page 129

2. Find out what's bugging him . . . . Page 130

3. Tell him that if he continues to ignore your instructions he'll be either transferred or dismissed . . . . . Page 133

Your answer: 1. There are too many interruptions.

You heard only one clue? But Joe gave others during his brief chat with you.

Please return and try again.

Your answer: 2. The equipment is faulty.

Is this all you heard? Maybe the equipment is old, but you'd better check out the other clues you got from your conversation with Joe. If there are other reasons for his poor performance, a new machine won't solve the problem.

Please try to hear a better answer.

Your answer: 3. Joe needs more training on the operation of
his machine.

There is more to hear than this. You could have gathered this
from Joe's remarks about the trouble he had feeding paper
into the machine. But other things were said, too, and if you
send Joe off for training before checking the other factors,
you may have solved only part of the problem.

Please return and listen again.

Your answer: 4. Answers one, two, and three.

Excellent hearing; the interruptions, the machine, and Joe's own ability (or lack of it) could all be barriers between Joe and good performance.

This is a good time to point out that the last several case histories have demonstrated how talking with the worker can be the most effective and satisfactory way of finding and removing barriers to good performance. Remember that it is important to be sure that the worker's goals are compatible with those of the company.

There are other situations, having nothing to do with the location and removal of barriers, in which talk does a great deal to help keep job performance at a high level. These are the situations in which you show that you recognize and acknowledge the importance of others. The least important person in the place needs to feel that he is of some value to the company, and a friendly hello now and then, a pleasant word or two here and there, or even just a nod and a smile will do more toward keeping people happy—and doing their best—than almost any other single thing you can think of. (This is true in private life, as well as in a job situation). The smile, the friendly word, are very simple things, and we tend to forget their power. Try not to forget.

We hope that you now have some insight into the importance of eliminating barriers and some of the ways it can be accomplished. Satisfying the needs and goals of individuals is an important means of reaching the company's goals.

For the next few pages we will review some of the ideas we have covered in this chapter. First, which of the following do you think keeps people from working in a continuously productive state?

1. Barriers to their performance . . . . Page 143

2. Their attitudes . . . . Page 144

Your answer: 5. Answers two and three.

You almost caught all the clues. These are important points;
Joe may need training or the equipment may be faulty. But
how about the number of interruptions? Is it just a gripe, or
are there actually too many?   Unless you check it out you
won't be sure.   It could be that neither a new machine nor
further training will improve Joe's performance enough by
itself.

Please return and hear the whole story.

Your answer: 1. Barriers to performance.

Correct. Barriers are the things that stand between a person and his goal.

Do you remember which type of conflict was described as representing a choice between two distasteful goals?

1. Avoidance-avoidance . . . . Page 145

2. Approach-avoidance . . . . Page 146

Your answer: 2. Their attitudes.

No. When people's attitudes toward a job situation are unhappy ones, it is usually because some barrier stands between
them and good job performance, as we have already
mentioned.

Please turn to page 143 for your next question.

Your answer: 1. Avoidance-avoidance.

You are correct. You recall that the three types of conflict situations were listed as:

Choice	*Behavior*
Between two desirable goals	approach-approach
Between a desirable goal and an undesirable goal	Approach-avoidance
Between two undesirable goals	Avoidance-avoidance

Next question: Do you think that lack of good working conditions is always a barrier to satisfactory performance?

1. Yes . . . . Page 147

2. No . . . . Page 148

Your answer: 2. Approach-avoidance.

No. Approach means going *toward* a desirable goal, not away from an undesirable goal.

You would have an avoidance-avoidance situation if you had to make a choice between two undesirable goals.

Please turn to page 145 for your next question.

Your answer: 1. Yes.

This is very doubtful. Certainly the working conditions would have to be exceptionally poor. Men have done surprising things under the most primitive conditions when they were properly motivated.

Barriers are, as we have said, those things that actually prevent a man from doing a good job. Such items as pay, the work itself, working conditions, benefits, and so on are not barriers; they are satisfiers or dissatisfiers, depending on the situation, but they do not actually keep a worker from doing a good job. They are often blamed for poor performance, however, while real barriers are left untouched.

On the other hand, poor equipment, poor instructions, and lack of skill all prevent satisfactory work no matter what the worker's motivation. Further, if these barriers are allowed to exist long enough, they cause attitudes in the worker which in themselves interfere with performance. Of course, not all barriers are as obvious as those mentioned above, but they do exist.

We hope that if you ever find yourself seeking out barriers to good performance you will look beyond working conditions, which will probably be no worse than dissatisfiers, to the real barriers.

Please proceed to page 149.

Your answer: 2. No.

Although the question can be debated, we think that this is the best answer. Working conditions, pay, the work itself, benefits, and so on are satisfiers if they satisfy and dissatisfiers if they do not. Even if they make a worker unhappy when he compares his lot with others, they still would not keep him from doing his best if he were motivated to do so.

On the other hand, poor equipment, poor instructions, and lack of skill all prevent satisfactory work no matter what the worker's motivation. Of course, not all barriers to good performance are as obvious as these. Some are much more difficult to see, though they are just as real.

We hope you chose this answer because you know the difference between dissatisfiers and barriers and are determined not to confuse them, as so many people do. If you ever have to seek out barriers to good performance, we know that you will look beyond working conditions.

Please proceed to page 149.

When you observe a person operating at a low level of performance, or whose behavior indicates something is wrong, what do you do?

1. Ignore the problem . . . . Page 150

2. Talk it over with him . . . . Page 151

Your answer: 1. Ignore the problem.

No, that's not right.

Some problems will take care of themselves, but few of them will take care of themselves the way we would want. The best way to ensure that future performance will be what we want is to find out what the problem is. This is much better than ignoring it.

Please proceed to page 151.

Your answer: 2. Talk it over with him.

Right! This is the best way to find solutions to the problems of people on the job. Get the problem out into the open and come to a solution.

Here is your last question.

You are trying to find out what barriers are keeping a man from doing well on the job. You try to discover what conflicts may exist, and you have made sure you know his goals and that he knows the company's goals and yours. While all this has been going on you have probably:

1. Tried to determine whether his attitudes were changing
   . . . . Page 152

2. Listened to what he had to say . . . . Page 153

3. Tried to make sure he wouldn't get upset . . . . Page 154

Your answer: 1. Tried to determine whether his attitudes were changing.

We hope not. This may have been your goal during the conversation but you'll never get there if you don't hear the man out (attitudes and all) as you listen to what he has to say.

Good listening offers us the reward of many clues to problems and their true sources. Learning to be a good listener is its own reward!

Please proceed to page 153.

Your answer: 2. Listen to what he has to say.

Good. That's the best answer.

Listening almost always pays off because we learn about the sources of problems, where barriers might really lie.

Please proceed now to page 155.

Your answer: 3. Try to make sure he doesn't get upset.

No. This is very considerate of you, but it's not the answer.

Being sure the man doesn't get upset might be your goal. In this case we doubt that you want to hear him out. Careful listening often brings out clues as to what's behind the problem or even to what it is. The closer you get to this point, the more upset the man may become.

However, chances are he won't get upset if you listen. In any case, give yourself the opportunity to hear what the conflict really is. That way you will have a much better feel for all the points to be considered before making a decision.

Try to learn to be a good listener.

Complete this brief test and then turn to the next page to check your answers. If you miss any of these questions, you can review the subject by going back to the pages indicated after the answers.

1. What do we call the things that get between a worker and his desire to do a good job?

2. Trying to decide the best action to take, or the best decision to make, can sometimes block a person from going toward a goal. When a person is faced with making a choice between two or more goals, he is faced with a _____ .

3. A person has fears and anxiety about his job. In this sense, fear and anxiety are _____ to productive performance.

4. You recognize that something is standing between a person and his best job performance. What is your first step?

5. The following is a list of actions to take when trying to uncover people's problems:
   a) Determine what stands between the man and his job.
   b) Get conflict out in the open.
   c) Listen not only to what is said but to what is behind what is said.
   d) Make certain that you both have the same goals.

What are we trying to accomplish when we take action as described in this list?

ANSWERS

1. Barriers (page 111)

2. Conflict (page 112, 116)

3. Barriers (page 122)

4. Have an informal discussion to compare viewpoints (page 123)

5. Finding and removing barriers to productive performance (page 128)

On page 157 you will find a brief list of books that deal at length and in detail with subjects covered in this text. They will prove to be useful references if you would like more information on managing with people.

Now please turn to page 163 and take the Post-Test.

READING LIST

Berelson, B., and G. A. Steiner, *Human Behavior,* Harcourt, Brace, and World, 1964.

Blake, R. R., and Jane S. Mouton, *The Managerial Grid,* Gulf Publishing Co., Houston, Texas, 1964.

Ingram, K. C., *Talk That Gets Results,* McGraw-Hill, New York, 1957.

Maslow, A. H., *Motivation and Personality,* Harper and Brothers, New York, 1954.

Nichols, R. G., and L. A. Stevens, *Are You Listening?* McGraw-Hill, New York, 1957.

Rush, H. M. F., *The Win-Lose Complex,* The Conference Board Record, June 1966.

PRE-TEST and POST-TEST

1. Man must satisfy his physical needs, such as those for food and water. He has other needs which are not physical but must also be satisfied. These are called _____ needs.

2. Which of the following needs is physical?

   a) Recognition   c) Water

   b) Affection   d) Security

3. A theory developed by A. H. Maslow classifies human needs as needs for the things listed below. Which of them do you think he considered the highest type of need?

   a) Social contact   d) Creativity

   b) Survival   e) Self-esteem

   c) Security

4. True or false: When the need for security is fulfilled, a person will feel safe.

5. The drive to satisfy one's needs always results in some kind of _____ .

   a) Motivation   b) Recognition   c) Behavior

6. Anything that attracts a person toward a goal is said to be _____ him.

159

7. A person seeking a goal is responding to an inner pressure called _____ .

8. True or false: The desire to be liked is a motive. _____

9. Select the best answer: The achiever likes _____ .
   a) Job challenges   d)   Answers (a) and (b)
   b) Immediate feedback   e)   Answers (a), (b), and (c)
   c) Risk taking

10. An elementary type of behavior is to seek _____ and avoid _____ .

11. Most adult behavior is _____ .
    a) Learned
    b) Instinctive

12. True or false: Things like raises or working conditions can be either satisfiers or dissatisfiers, depending on our expectations.

13. When examining factors that contribute to motivation, you should look first at _____ .
    a) What you expect of the worker
    b) What the worker expects of the job

14. Things that block a worker from doing a good job are called _____ .

15. Giving poor instructions or not listening to problems can create _____ barriers.

    a) Physical

    b) Mental

16. True or false: Having not enough paid holidays is a barrier to good performance.

17. What is the first step to take when you have decided that something is keeping a worker from doing his job satisfactorily? _____

    _____

18. When talking things over with a worker for the purpose of solving his problem, your most important function is to _____ .

    a) Make him feel at ease

    b) Listen to what he says

    c) Explain your viewpoint

(Answers to this test can be found on page 167)

POST-TEST

1. Man must satisfy his physical needs, such as those for food and water. He has other needs which are not physical but must also be satisfied. These are called _____ needs.

2. Which of the following needs is physical?
   a) Recognition
   c) Water
   b) Affection
   d) Security

3. A theory developed by A. H. Maslow classifies human needs as needs for the things listed below. Which of them do you think he considered the highest type of need?

   _____

   a) Social contact
   d) Creativity
   b) Survival
   e) Self-esteem
   c) Security

4. True or false: When the need for security is fulfilled, a person will feed safe.

5. The drive to satisfy one's needs always results in some kind of_____ .
   a) Motivation   b) Recognition   c) Behavior

6. Anything that attracts a person toward a goal is said to be_____ him.

7.   A person seeking a goal is responding to an inner pressure called _____ .

8.   True or false: The desire to be liked is a motive. _____

9.   Select the best answer: The achiever likes _____ .
     a) Job challenges   d)   Answers (a) and (b)
     b) Immediate feedback   e)   Answers (a), (b), and (c)
     c) Risk taking

10. An elementary type of behavior is to seek _____ and avoid _____ .

11. Most adult behavior is _____ .
     a) Learned
     b) Instinctive

12. True or false: Things like raises or working conditions can be either satisfiers or dissatisfiers, depending on our expectations.

13. When examining factors that contribute to motivation, you should look first at _____ .
     a) What you expect of the worker
     b) What the worker expects of the job

14. Things that block a worker from doing a good job are called _____ .

15. Giving poor instructions or not listening to problems can create _____ barriers.

   a) Physical

   b) Mental

16. True or false: Having not enough paid holidays is a barrier to good performance.

17. What is the first step to take when you have decided that something is keeping a worker from doing his job satisfactorily? _____

   _____

18. When talking things over with a worker for the purpose of solving his problem, your most important function is to _____ .

   a) Make him feel at ease

   b) Listen to what he says

   c) Explain your viewpoint

(Answers to this test can be found on page 167)

TEST ANSWERS

1. Mental (or emotional)

2. (c) Water

3. (d) Creativity

4. False

5. (c) Behavior

6. Motivating

7. Drive

8. True

9. (e) Answers (a), (b), and (c)

10. Reward/punishment (or pleasure/pain)

11. (a) Learned

12. True

13. (b) What the worker expects of the job

14. Barriers (or obstructions)

15. (b) Mental

16. False

17. Talk things over with him to find out what the trouble is.

18. (b) Listen to what he says